ATLANTA FALCONS

RICHARD RAMBECK

CREATIVE EDUCATION INC.

Published by Creative Education, Inc.
123 S. Broad Street, Mankato, Minnesota 56001

Designed by Rita Marshall
Cover illustration by Lance Hidy Associates
Photos by Allsport, Sportschrome, Wide World Photos, Duomo, Focus On Sports and Spectra-Action

Copyright © 1991 Creative Education, Inc.
International copyrights reserved in all countries.
No part of this book may be reproduced in any form without written permission from the publisher.
Printed in the United States of America

Library of Congress Cataloging-in-Publication Data

Rambeck, Richard.
   Atlanta Falcons/Richard Rambeck.
   p.   cm.
   ISBN 0-88682-359-5
  1. Atlanta Falcons (Football team)—History.   I. Title.
GV956.A85R36   1990
796.332′64′09758231—dc20   90-41078
                                       CIP

In the South, all roads lead to Atlanta, or at least it seems that way. Atlanta is the capital of Georgia, and it is one of the largest cities in the South. It is also the hub of the region, much as New York City is the hub of the Northeast and Los Angeles is the hub of the West.

Atlanta has always been the jewel of the South. To this day, many southerners can't forgive what the Union troops did to the city during the Civil War. Union General Sherman and his men marched through Georgia in 1864 and practically burned Atlanta to the ground. But the city recovered, and it has built itself up to retain its vital role in the region.

In 1966, Tommy Nobis led a charging Falcon defense.

1 9 6 5

Atlanta who? "Falcons!" suggested a Georgia school teacher because of their courage, fight, and sporting tradition.

It is not surprising, then, that Atlanta is home to the oldest southern-based team in the National Football League. The Atlanta Falcons, started playing in the 1966 season, becoming the fifteenth team in the NFL. The Falcons flew into battle with the support of the entire city. The team sold 45,000 season tickets several months before it ever played a game.

When the team finally took the field, in September 1966, the fans were not only determined to cheer their Falcons to victory, they were prepared to cheer, no matter what. They cheered long incomplete passes by the Falcons. They cheered the team when it left the field at halftime. They cheered, and cheered, and cheered.

Despite the cheering, the Falcons struggled, and struggled, and struggled. Since the team's formation in 1966, Atlanta has won only one division title. The Falcons have made the playoffs only three times in their history and have won only one playoff game. Despite that record, Atlanta fans have had hopes of making it to the Super Bowl, especially in 1981, the year after the Falcons won their only division title. Those hopes were dashed, but the fans in Atlanta keep believing in their team, keep believing their team is ready for prime time.

Now, entering their twenty-fifth season, the Falcons are ready for prime time—or rather Prime Time. Prime Time is the nickname of Deion Sanders, a defensive back and punt returner who gave Atlanta fans a lot to cheer about during his rookie season. Sanders is a flashy, talented performer who may help bring Atlanta what it has always wanted—a championship.

Defenders like Sanders and John Case (#25) led Atlanta into the nineties.

NOBIS KNOCKS HEADS

1 9 6 6

Linebacker Tommy Nobis was the Falcons' first representative in the Pro Bowl.

Sanders is hardly Atlanta's first star. The club has always had players who were among the best in the NFL, even from the beginning. The first player the Falcons ever picked in the college draft was a hard-nosed linebacker from the University of Texas, Tommy Nobis. At Texas, Nobis was a true star. Both Texas pro teams—the Houston Oilers and the Dallas Cowboys—desperately wanted Nobis. So did their fans.

One Oiler lover, a man named Frank Boorman, sent Nobis an urgent message, begging the linebacker to sign with Houston. That wasn't unusual. Players as good as Nobis receive messages like that all the time. But this was no ordinary message. Boorman, you see, was an astronaut, and his message to Nobis was sent from space.

But Boorman didn't get his wish. Atlanta drafted Nobis, and he agreed to sign with the first-year team. What the Falcons got was a player who loved to hit people as hard as he could. "I hit 'em right in the goozle—high and hard," Nobis said. "That way they don't go anywhere but down."

And they went down a lot. Nobis dominated the Falcon defense. He was a one-man wrecking crew. In his book "The Professionals," author Ray Didinger writes this about Nobis:

"He was great long before the Atlanta Falcons were good. An expansion team, the Falcons were stocked mostly by free agents and castoffs from other clubs. Nobis virtually was a one-man defense. Hal Herring, the Falcons defensive coach, kept a chart on rookie tackles that season

[1966]. In his first 12 games, Nobis had 150 tackles and 103 assists. That meant he was on top of the ball carrier 21 times a game—or one-third of the plays!"

Led by Nobis, the Falcons actually won three games their first season and managed to avoid last place. Their three victories came in the final five games. Atlanta defeated the New York Giants (27-16), Minnesota Vikings (20-13), and St. Louis Cardinals (16-10). The win over the Cardinals destroyed St. Louis's playoff hopes. The triumph over the Giants sent the New York team tumbling into last place.

The future looked bright. The Falcons were young and were bound to improve. Nobis, quarterback Randy Johnson, running back Junior Coffey, and wide receiver Alex Hawkins all seemed destined for greatness. So did their team. But the Falcons fell flat on their tail feathers in 1967. They won only one game, against Minnesota.

Nobis, typically, played a big role in the victory. His tackles helped hold the Vikings to twenty points, but it was his running ability that set up the winning score. Nobis recovered a fumble and ran deep into Minnesota territory. Johnson then guided the Falcons to a touchdown and a 21-20 victory.

After the 1-13 season, one sportswriter said the Falcons, with one exception, should all jump into the nearby Savannah River. The exception was Tommy Nobis.

The following year, the Falcons changed coaches and drafted another defensive star. The new coach was former pro quarterback Norm Van Brocklin. The new defensive standout was end Claude Humphrey from Tennessee

1 9 6 7

September 17: The Colts defeat the Falcons despite an Atlanta club record 99 yard kickoff return.

Tough defense has always been a trademark of Atlanta football. (pages 10–11)

1 9 6 9

Part of a powerful defensive squad, Steve Szezecko (#71) joins in to stop Gale Sayers.

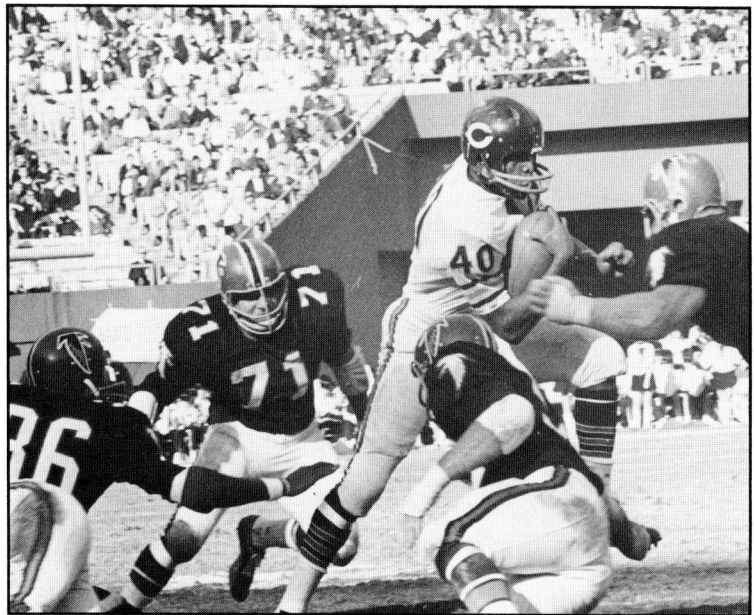

State. Humphrey and Nobis teamed up to give Atlanta an outstanding defense. Humphrey, in fact, was named NFL Rookie of the Year in 1968.

Humphrey liked to try to intimidate opposing players, particularly quarterbacks. "I'm going to run you out of the league," he growled to Baltimore Colt quarterback John Unitas. Run Unitas out of the league? That was pretty tough talk for a mere rookie, especially since Unitas was considered a superstar. But Humphrey backed up his words with a series of ferocious tackles against the Colts.

In 1969, Van Brocklin's coaching and the fine play of Nobis and Humphrey led the Falcons to a franchise-record six victories, including a big win over the Minnesota Vikings, the team that had fired Van Brocklin. The Falcons continued to improve under Van Brocklin. In 1973 the team gained first place with an 8-3 record, but the season wasn't over. The Falcons still needed two wins to make the playoffs. Instead, they lost two straight. Van Brocklin never was able to build the team up again. Once more the Falcons needed a new star.

FALCONS SEE BARTKOWSKI AS A SAVIOR

What the Falcons had to have was a great quarterback, something the team had always lacked. In 1966, Atlanta used the first pick in the college draft to take Tommy Nobis. Nine years later, the Falcons had the first pick again. This time they took a quarterback: a tall, good-looking Californian named Steve Bartkowski, who had a rifle for an arm.

Running back Dave Hampton became the first Falcon to gain 1,000 yards on the ground.

Bartkowski was not only good, he was confident. At the University of California, he set every passing record, leading his college team to its best record in more than ten years. As a senior, he was named to virtually every All-America team. He was the All-American boy, and Atlanta fans thought he was the player to lead the Falcons to the promised land—the Super Bowl. Bartkowski didn't mind the attention or the expectations. In fact, he loved them. "I enjoyed reading about myself. I enjoyed picking up the paper and reading that I was the savior," Bartkowski said. "I really thought I could walk in here and turn this team around overnight."

At first, though, Bartkowski wasn't a savior. In fact, he wasn't even a star. The young quarterback made a lot of mistakes. The Falcons finished with a 4-10 record in both of his first two seasons. The team had a long way to go to get to the Super Bowl. In 1977, a new coach, Leeman Bennett, was named to lead the Falcons. Bennett, who was

Falcons defense soared to NFL record by allowing just 129 points in 14 games.

only thirty-nine at the time, was the youngest coach in the NFL. Despite an injury to Bartkowski that caused him to miss most of the 1977 season, the Falcons went 7-7. Hopes were high again.

In 1978 Bartkowski returned, determined to prove that he was, indeed, a star. But a miserable showing in a preseason game earned Bartkowski a seat on the sideline. The young coach had benched his young quarterback. In the locker room after the game, Bartkowski sat and cried.

But Bennett hadn't given up on Bartkowski. Even though Bartkowski was no longer a starter, Bennett made sure that Bartkowski got a lot of attention during practice. It was as if Bennett were saying, "You're not our quarterback now, but you will be. Just work on getting better." It was difficult for Bartkowski. He had never failed like this, not in high school or college. He wasn't the star, and that was hard for him to take.

Bartkowski loved the limelight. He loved making a lot of money. He loved driving fast cars. And he loved being surrounded by beautiful women. But now, as a bench sitter, none of this mattered to Bartkowski. His outlook changed: he stopped being a playboy and became very religious. He was determined to become a good person and a good leader for the Falcons. "I have a motto: If you don't stand for something, you'll fall for anything," Bartkowski said.

He stopped thinking about being a star and started trying to get better. Of his benching, Bartkowski said, "That was the lowest I've been in my life, and it was the best thing that ever happened to me."

Bartkowski regained the starting job before the fifth game of the 1978 season. He led the team to a 9-7 record

Atlanta quarterback Steve Bartkowski.

Steve Bartkowski set a new Falcon record by passing for 324 yards against Denver.

and a spot in the playoffs; it was the first time the team had taken part in postseason play. In the first round of the playoffs, the Falcons faced the Philadelphia Eagles in Atlanta. The Falcons fell behind 13-0, but the Atlanta fans, who had waited more than ten years to see their heroes in a playoff game, kept roaring their support. Bartkowski put together two late touchdown drives, and the Falcons defeated Philadelphia 14-13.

Atlanta was now two steps away from the Super Bowl. The following week in Dallas, the Falcons fought gamely against the powerful Cowboys. But Dallas held off the determined Atlanta team 27-20. Dallas went on to make it into the Super Bowl. Although Atlanta's journey stopped two victories short of the Super Bowl, hopes were sky-high for 1979.

ANDREWS RUSHES IN

The Falcons did not make it to the Super Bowl in 1979. In fact, they didn't even get into the playoffs or have a winning season. But they found a new star, a tough, hard-nosed running back named William Andrews. He came to Atlanta from Auburn University. At Auburn, Andrews wasn't a star running back. He was a running back who spent most of his time blocking for teammate Joe Cribbs, who would be drafted by the Buffalo Bills.

When Andrews arrived at training camp, the Falcons were hoping that he could block for teammate Lynn Cain, who had been a star running back at the University of Southern California. Andrews impressed Coach Bennett in preseason practice, not only with his ability to block, but with his ability to run with the ball. It didn't take

Lynn Cain (#21) teamed with Andrews to form a powerful backfield. (page 17)

Steve Bartkowski led a fast paced Falcon offense. (pages 18–19)

1 9 8 0

William Andrews (right) rushed for over 1,300 yards to lead the Falcon offense.

Bennett and the rest of the coaches long to realize that they had more than a blocker on their hands—they had a great runner.

Andrews gained more than 100 yards in each of his first two regular season games with Atlanta. At the end of the season, Andrews had established a new team rushing record with 1,023 yards. Andrews achieved his success with a unique style: he ran slightly bent over with his head lowered. "I try to stay lower than my opponent," Andrews said, "come at him in a ball and then . . ." And then, BOOM! Andrews ran over a lot of guys who were a lot bigger than he was. Soon, William Andrews had a reputation as the hardest-hitting running back in the NFL.

Andrews had a great rookie season in 1979, but he had even a better year in 1980. He rushed for more than 1,300 yards and caught passes for another 736 yards. He became one of the few running backs in NFL history to gain more than 2,000 combined rushing and pass-catching yards.

With Andrews leading the way on the ground and Bartkowski having his best year as a pro, the Falcons went 12-4 in 1980 and won the National Football Conference's Western Division. In addition, they finished the regular season with the best record in the National Football Conference.

In the first round of the playoffs, the Falcons met the Dallas Cowboys in Atlanta. Two years earlier, Dallas had destroyed Atlanta's Super Bowl hopes with a playoff game victory over the Falcons. Atlanta was determined to even the score. After all, the Falcons were at home in front of their loyal, loud fans. Bartkowski and Andrews led the team to a 27-17 lead midway through the fourth quarter. It appeared that the Falcons were only minutes away from advancing to the conference title game; Dallas, though, had other plans.

William Andrews averaged a record setting 4.9 yards per carry during the season.

The Cowboys were perhaps the best comeback team in pro football. The Falcons fought hard to hold off a Dallas rally, but a late touchdown pass from Danny White to Drew Pearson gave the Cowboys a 30-27 victory. Atlanta's best season ever was over, but hopes remained high.

Unfortunately, the Falcons never could duplicate the success they had in 1980. In fact, they had losing seasons in 1981 and 1982. Despite the defeats, Andrews just got better and better. He played in the Pro Bowl four straight years, and he had the respect of all of his opponents. "He is just the best runner in the NFL," said Buffalo linebacker Jim Haslett. "I know all about Walter Payton, Tony Dorsett, Eric Dickerson, and the rest. But Andrews is the best I've seen."

Atlanta's all-time leading rusher, William Andrews.

If Andrews was one of the best players on the field, he was also one of the best citizens off the field. He devoted much of his free time to charity work of all kinds. His motto was, "If you've got time to talk to me, I've got time to talk to you." Andrews always had a smile on his face and a warm greeting. He always looked on the positive side of a situation. "William Andrews can catch fish even when they won't bite," said Atlanta defensive line coach Tom Brasher.

But Andrews's string of successful seasons ended in 1984. During a preseason scrimmage that year, Andrews got a handoff from Bartkowski and started up the middle. He was caught from behind and something in his knee snapped. He was carried off the field with one of the worst knee injuries in NFL history. Not only was the knee damaged, the muscles around the knee were torn up as well. Andrews sat out two full seasons trying to get back into shape. When he finally returned, in 1986, every Falcon greeted him as a hero. But this hero wasn't what he used to be. He wasn't as strong, he wasn't as powerful, and he wasn't as hard to tackle. Soon after his comeback, Andrews retired as Atlanta's all-time leading rusher.

September 2: 202 yards rushing in 35 carries propelled Gerald Riggs into the Atlanta record books.

PRIME TIME AND THE FALCONS

Atlanta struggled throughout the 1980s. Bartkowski and Andrews finished their NFL careers on losing teams. The Falcons changed coaches several times, but none of them was able to guide the team to success. In 1987, Atlanta drafted a young, promising quarterback named Chris Miller. He had a good rookie season until he was hurt. Miller also had injury problems in 1988 and

Quarterback Chris Miller rebounded from injuries to rank as the NFL's seventh best passer.

1989. The Falcons' losing records meant they had high choices—usually in the top five—in the NFL draft. This is a way to get good young players. In the 1989 draft, the Falcons got a player who is as good as they come.

When Deion Sanders was in college at Florida State, he always stood out in a crowd. On the field, he was a gifted defensive back and punt returner who was capable of breaking any game open with one big play. Off the field, Sanders liked to rent limousines and dress up in expensive tuxedos. He also wore jewelry—a lot of jewelry. Much of it was made out of gold; all of it was expensive. Sanders also had a flashy nickname: Prime Time. "I am Prime Time," he said to anyone who called him Deion. When Sanders played in enemy stadiums, the fans booed him constantly. He was too flashy, they thought. In one road game against Clemson University, Sanders returned a punt for a touchdown. Once he got to the end zone, Sanders turned to the fans who had been booing him the whole game and yelled, "How do you like me now?" The fans responded by booing even louder, but it was Sanders who had the last laugh. Florida State beat Clemson.

When the Falcons drafted Sanders in 1989, it appeared they would never be able to sign him. Sanders and his agent made it known that Atlanta would have to pay Sanders a fortune or they would lose him to Sanders's other love—baseball. While in college, Sanders spent his summers playing baseball in the New York Yankees organization. The Yankees considered him a future star and said they were willing to pay Sanders a lot of money to be a baseball player instead of a football player.

While Sanders's agent and the Falcons tried to agree on a contract, Sanders played with the Yankees. One night in

Seattle, Sanders and the Yankees were playing the Seattle Mariners. Sanders hit a home run and then returned to the dugout. "You have a phone call," one of the New York assistant coaches told him. It was Sanders's agent, and he had good news for Deion. The Falcons had offered a multi-million-dollar contract. The agent said yes, and Prime Time was a Falcon. One inning after hitting the homer, Sanders was saying goodbye to his Yankee teammates. He left Seattle on a jet within an hour, heading south.

Triple threat! Newcomer Deion Sanders led the team in punt returns, kick-off returns and interceptions.

When Sanders arrived in Atlanta, he spoke to reporters and told them not to call him "Neon." That was the nickname some teammates had given him at Florida State, and Sanders didn't like it. "That just doesn't sound like me," he said. He insisted on being called Prime Time. When the other Falcons saw Sanders with all his jewelry and expensive clothes, they wondered if Sanders had an attitude problem. Would he be a loud-mouthed rookie who would show no respect for the veteran players? They didn't have to worry. In fact, if they wanted to know about the real Deion Sanders, all they had to do was talk to his mother, Connie Knight. Connie knows Deion is basically a quiet guy off the field. She also knows that the jewelry is all for show.

"When Deion's around me, he knows better than to wear that junk. He only likes to flash that stuff for the pictures," Connie Knight said.

Once Sanders started practicing with the Falcons, his new teammates noticed something else about him. Sanders works hard, and he hits hard. "I've never seen a guy with such athletic ability," said Atlanta defensive backfield coach Fred Bruney. "And Deion throws his body around like it was somebody else's." Ex-Falcon head coach Marion

The Atlanta defense prepares to immobilize the Cardinals. (pages 26–27)

1 9 9 0

The flamboyant and athletic Deion Sanders (right) inspired the Falcons.

Campbell was immediately impressed with Sanders's ability to make big plays. "He's a takeaway guy, a weapon," Campbell said.

In his first regular season game with the Falcons, Sanders proved just how big a weapon he is. Against the Los Angeles Rams, he caught a punt, then dropped it. With Ram tacklers bearing down on him, Sanders easily picked up the ball, raced to his right, broke about four tackles and went seventy yards for a touchdown. "In twenty-seven years in this league, I've never experienced the buzz that goes through a stadium when this guy gets near the football," Campbell said. Sanders was so good, the Falcons were determined to find other ways to use him. They even had him playing wide receiver in one game his rookie year.

One of the Falcons' dynamic new stars, Shawn Collins.

The tough and dependable John Settle.

Ex-Houston Oiler coach Jerry Glanville began his second year as the Atlanta field general.

Every time Sanders made a big play, and he made a lot of them in 1989, he would celebrate after the play with a dance and some finger-pointing. Atlanta fans loved it; fans in other stadiums hated it. But they all wanted to see Prime Time. "Some people will come out to see me do well," Sanders said. "Some people will come out to see me get run over. But love me or hate me, they're going to come to see me play."

Players like Sanders and Chris Miller are again providing hope for Atlanta fans. The Falcons didn't have a good record in 1989, but they showed they have some of the best young talent in the NFL. They also have a new coach, Jerry Glanville, who made the Houston Oilers into a winning team.

When Glanville got to Houston, the Oilers had far less talent than the Falcons do now. With the Falcons, Glanville has a defensive star in Sanders and an offensive star in Miller. There are also plenty of good players at other positions, especially offensive tackle Bill Fralic, who is one of the best in the league. Following behind Fralic's blocking is John Settle a tough young running back who has his eyes on the Falcon record book.

As they enter their twenty-fifth season, in 1990, the Falcons finally believe they have what they need to be a championship team. In other words, the Falcons and Deion "Prime Time" Sanders are ready for prime time.

Heterick Memorial Library
Ohio Northern University

DUE	RETURNED	DUE	RETURNED
1.		13.	
2.		14.	
3.		15.	
4.		16.	
5.		17.	
6.		18.	
7.		19.	
8.		20.	
9.		21.	
10.		22.	
11.		23.	
12.		24.	

WITHDRAWN FROM
OHIO NORTHERN
UNIVERSITY LIBRARY

HETERICK MEMORIAL LIBRARY

3 5111 00396 7407